THE QUEST

Kenn Amaechi Jnr.

THE QUEST

Kenn Amaechi Jnr.

Kenn Amaechi Jnr.

Copyright ©2015 Kenn Amaechi Jnr.

ISBN: 978-978-952-751-9

All rights reserved.
No part of this book may be reproduced, distributed, stored in a retrieval system or transmitted, in any form or by any means, electronic, electrostatic, magnetic tape, mechanical, photocopying, recording or otherwise without prior written permission from the Publisher.
For information about permission to reproduce selections from this book, write to info@wrr.ng

National Library of Nigeria Cataloguing-in-Publication Data

Printed and Published in Nigeria by:

Words Rhymes & Rhythm Limited
Suite C309, Global Plaza Plot 366, Obafemi Awolowo Way, Jabi District, Abuja, Nigeria.

08169027757, 08060109295
www.wrr.ng

The Quest

CONTENTS

DEDICATION	7
PREFACE	8
COMMENTS	10
LIFE	12
LIFE (II)	14
THE QUEST	17
SHREDS	18
SHREDS	18
LOST	20
BEAUTIFUL SACRILEGE	21
IN THEIR DEFENCE	23
NOT MY SONG	25
APOCALYPSE	27
THE GOOD SHEPHERD	28
TELL THEM	30
TAKE ME THERE	32
TAKE ME THERE II	33
TAKE ME THERE III	34
GIVE ME A SONG	35
I SEEK YOU	36
I SEE YOU	38
LOVE TO LOVE YOU	39
TOUCH MY HEART	41
THE PERFECT CURATOR	42
IN AWE OF YOU	44
ETERNAL LOVE	45
LOVE	47

TIME FLIGHT 49
TIME MESSAGE 50
TWILIGHT 52
NATURE 53
NIGHT II 54
BIRTH TO DEATH 55
RICHES IN LIMBO 56
BLISS OF PARADISE 57
DEATH OF AN EMPIRE 58
MY HERO 59
HAPPINESS IN CREATIVITY 60
I WEPT 61
I LEARN WITH TEARS 63
POCKET YOUR ANGER 65
AIDS 67
BEAST OF EXTINCTION 68
CARO 69
NKOSI JOHNSON 71
CHAOS CITY (I) 72
CHAOS CITY (II) 73
OSHODI 74
BURNING FLAME 75
EVERGREEN 76
FARE WELL TO MAMA 77
THE PRECIPICE 78
SILENT WISHES 79
FRAGRANCE OF LOVE 80
THE MOMENT I BEHELD THEE 81

The Quest

NIGHT 82
SHADOWS 84
SONG FOR MYSELF 86
REMINISCENCES 88
WHEN I WAS A CHILD 90
I WANT TO HEAR A LULLABY 91
CHILDHOOD PARADISE 92
HISTORIANS 95
ADIEU HISTORIANS 97
SUNSET 99
AMIN AL-MUMINI 101
AKACHI 103
SERVICE TO THE FATHER LAND 105
THE LIVING SPRING 107
EXPECT GREAT THINGS 109
LET'S MAKE A CHOICE 110
I AM A BANKER 112
ME 113

Kenn Amaechi Jnr.

DEDICATION

To my mum Late Mrs. Bridget Amaechi who sacrificed her life for the love she believed in. May your Soul find true love and peace eternal.

The Quest

PREFACE

Life is a quest for everything in life which is nothing in death,
The sun like the balloon is indifferent to the vagaries of human quest,
Like the sun our quest rises and exits at its setting:
Life is a quest for everything in life which is nothing in death.

THE QUEST is a distinct breed of poetry. It was originally conceived under ***ECHOES OF CONSCIENCE*** another literary work by the author. It however birthed its own course to follow its on rhythms.

The collections of the quest it's a salad bowl of soul searching, heart touching and emotionally charming condiments of pure altruistic poetic and philosophical lines rendered from the bosom of a pure innocence.

The poems mirror and express the innate striving of man to achieve happiness by setting himself free from life transient and unpredictable nature and thus live a life devoid of fear and all spiritual and temporal abstractions.

The themes of the poem are varied with the seasons of their birth, with an incubation period of nine years from (1997-2006). The quest is a song, singed at a time when all motives for cosmetics have been removed from the poets mind.

The reader will find out that the major connecting thread of the poems is the quest for answer to ideas, matters and principalities that tends to influence his life. The quest to know, the quest to be free, the quest for self expression, the quest for happiness and love, the quest to do good and avoid evil and the quest to walk with his creator in compassion.

The quest does not end at that as the odds and demands of life bore yet another quest for his childhood years of virgin innocence years of bliss, years uncensored by common sense. As the wants of man is endless so also is his ques.

Kenn Amaechi Jnr.

Some of the poems are mere poetic statements and the poet claims no superior poetic prowess than what is presented. Additionally the reader will find out that the poems are not hidden in any esoteric poetic language or obscure poetic devices.

The poems are meant to be simply read and simply understood without scuffles. Be it as it may some of the poems are the poet's experiences, caricatures, thoughts and feelings which are poetically crafted for reading pleasure. It's a kind of relief to life multifaceted pan demonic theatre.

I humbly wish this literary work adds value to our lives and put smiles on our faces.

The sun like the balloon is in different to the vagaries of human quest,

Like the sun our quest rises and exits at its setting
Life is a maze in which we take the wrong
Steps before we learnt to walk...

The wise one said all the quests of mankind are
nothing but vanity upon vanity which end in vanity.

The Quest

COMMENTS

The Quest is a satirical mirror of our society, a tale of our earnest quest and unspoken fantasies, a reflection of Man's thirst for goodness, affection, perfection, and charity amidst a cloud of malevolence.
It is a collection of poems for truth seekers, God lovers, children, and adults. At the heart of this book, is a good, relaxing, and relatable read. The wisdom expressed is deep for the discerning. The author's personal narratives are beautifully crafted for our collective delight and insight. Thanks Ken for this immortal gift.
Nwamaka Anaza
Assistant Professor and Educator, Southern ILLINOIS University Carbondale, U.S.A

This is a sound scholastic contribution from a young and highly promising intellectual. To say so much in a very little way is not a mean achievement.
This is a work for all to own.
Dr. Ibrahim Maina Waziri
Department of History, University of Maiduguri

It is truly amazing to see such a beautiful compilation of poems from a young man like Kenn Amaechi Jr am simply impressed.
Dr. Izzat Ullah
Lecturer Faculty of Law, University of Maiduguri

Ken Amaechi Jr has a revolution in his heart and this shows in the poems he has penned
A burning desire not only to paint the gray arrears of the lives we live, but to push us to aspire to   loftier ideals.
Chika Jones Onwuasoanya
Renowned spoken word poet, Co-author of 'VERSES FROM THE NIGER'

Kenn Amaechi Jnr.

The quest echoes…

life is empty
      life is full
life is poor
      life is rich
life is cruel
      life is kind
life is sweet
      life is sweat
life is ugly

LIFE IS BEAUTIFUL!

The Quest

LIFE

Life?
A hermaphrodites
Which made me
A victim
of the jungle faces
of humanity.

Life!
which tells me much
yet leaves me
groping for the unreal.

I have been a victim
of moral jacket
and conscientious coats
My good measures
have measured
me down
the length
of an ant.

I can't
be overwhelmed
defiantly
I embalmed stoicism
To clear away
the cloud
of doubt and pessimism
that blankets
My vision
of this life.
Should I be dismayed
I resolved
not to be overcome
oblivion
I trust a shield

Kenn Amaechi Jnr.

Against the
tyranny of innocence.

I sing
Lamentations
of the cheating of nature
Life itself
is a mirage.
Now!
that I can see
beyond the two extremes
I will carry them along
each with its own
wage and cross
To bear own burdens
the good and bad
shared equally amongst
its kiths and kins
in life's
multifaceted
pandemonic
theatre.   (August 1998)

"*Man should be bewailed at their birth and not their death*" –
Montesquieu

The Quest

LIFE (II)

I have been indifferent
to the smoldering worries
of mankind
life is simple
life is sweet
life is sweat
life is swell
when you learn to eat
what comes your way
And do all those deeds
that please your heart.
When homeless,
sleep soundly
under the bridge
with mosquitoes and cold
whispering
     life is beautiful
When the urge to ease out
I do so, I count no days
nor do I cling to etiquettes
I search not for morality
In volume of voidness
At the sound of music
My feet shuffles for motion
To God my worship
praise to my fellows
is my daily anthem
Right and wrong
aint my resting bed
though I try to lay on the right
But on convenience I lay on the wrong
a little to the right
a little to the left
I don't sit
on the fence
I readily jump over
to moon shade side
Whenever the sunshade

Kenn Amaechi Jnr.

Gets too hot,
I fly for safety
to cold quarters
in compromise
score is settled.
none does wrong
all does right
I see no evil
I think no evil
    but
don't cajole me

I have seen
a man
out of worry
worry his life
to an early grave
Where as he couldn't
help his worry
his worries
helped him
to six feet, beneath earth's beautiful surface.
I have seen
Some labor
Themselves to death
while others
with pen
    paper
and a scent of faith and luck
Ride on the world's treasure

The sun is bright
The sun is dark
How you look at it
So it seems.

I have seen
a man
who out of spite
asked to be crucified

The Quest

like Christ
he died unhallowed, unknown, unjustified
one set to know everything
but end up
knowing not himself.

.

Another fresh with ideas
turned his wears backward,
an opening in the chest
A hole on the buttocks for air
Unzipped zippers down below
Some thoughts
It's the trend
And followed the craze
And there goes
a maddening crowd
in a maddening world.

Life is empty
life is full
life is poor
life is rich
life is sweet
life is sweat
life is ugly
life is beautiful.

(January 1998)

"Life is an ocean, anyone who put both feet's down at the same time will definitely drown" – Unknown

Kenn Amaechi Jnr.

THE QUEST

Life is a quest

For everything in life
That is nothing in death
The quest a search
For abstract realities
That never becomes
The sun like the balloon
Is indifferent to the vagaries
Of human quest
Like the sun
Our quest rises
And exits
At its setting.

(January 2003)

"Vanity upon vanity all is vanity..." – *King Solomom*

The Quest

SHREDS

A cloud over the universe
a blanket against cold war
an air that suffocates our reasons
and moulds us into
time-floating waves
      peace
           peace
                  peace
every where but nowhere
in the homes and street place?
under the shelter
of the minarets and the spires?
within the serenity
of flowing rivers and lakes?
under the umbrella
of the thick forest?
in the sugar-coated speeches
of the enthusiastic philosophers?

Peace
the sweet songs of moral painters
the chorus of sycophantic fools
the chants of the naïve multitudes
the cloth over wretched souls
    where can you be found?
    Deceitful brotherhood
    of freedom and liberty

Where are you hidden?
    Sure
not in the clan of blood-thirsty gluttons
not in the tribe of war-mongers
not in the lineage of breeders of animosity
not in the tongue that spits
fire and consumes innocent men
and certainly notin the ephemeral tongue twisted honesty
of well flavoured speeches
that has corrugated

Kenn Amaechi Jnr.

the soul of decent men
and left us with a world
      (January 1999)
spilt from the middle
into un-peaceful shreds.

"If you deny justice then you must live with crises, if you deny peace then you must live with violence" – John F Kennedy

The Quest

LOST

    They are parents
    That have lost their parenthood
    Children that have
     Lost their innocence
     Friends that have lost
     Their friendships
     Lovers that lives
       In parallel world
       All lost
       To the smoldering smoke
       Of cigarette
             And
             Hemp
       Which have like the wind
       Dispersed them away
       To the wonderland
       Of insanity.

**Written in September 2002 for Hamisu, a secondary school mate lost to the smoldering smoke of marijuana insanity.

Kenn Amaechi Jnr.

BEAUTIFUL SACRILEGE

The ceremony
Was every ones dream
The joy reached the heavens
The sun stood still
Until showers of ecstasy
poured like rain on the celebrant
The hand of the almighty
Was truly manifest
In the matrimony
Of the osu and diala
    Yet
It was a sacrilege,
The land has been defiled
And a taboo committed
    Yet
The gods and priest
Of the land
Stood castrate
Watching
Weakling
While
Its daughter
Radiate love
In the embrace
Of the osu clan

Every body came
Every body ate
Every body drank
Every body dance
To cupid sanctimonious sanction
As we behold
A beautiful garland
Of the creatures
Might over man
Ugly only in the eyes
Of mammon's

The Quest

And stone men in civilized age.
(September 2005)

***Written against the Igbo tradition that prohibits marriage between "a free born" and an "Osu" Caste. Even though the Supreme Court has ruled against such caste segregation, it still persists.*

"Tradition is an ancient slave master that is jealous of the liberty of its servants, its chain is often difficult to brake its adherents are bound to its bondage" – Kenn Amaechi Jnr.

Kenn Amaechi Jnr.

IN THEIR DEFENCE

I
A product of eager organs
Music hungry to taste
And hear the tone
Of their fertile sensitivities

Their music a rhythm
To stricken stone flesh
A cantonment of un-satiated bones
In consonance with liquid orchestra
Echoing volume of penetrable insanities
Which roars and ughs – hums
From the beating bands
Of a turgid stick and boiling hymen
That tipped up the earth's balance
With sacrilegious vibrations
Gyrating in ecstatic satisfaction
Of nature's desires –
I am now crucified for what I knew not
Hanged for a sin that preceded my creation
I, a by-product of un-hypocritical pleasure,
Journey to heavenly climax.

Had I known
I would have scattered your seed
And be not your evil spawn
But who am I to fight nature?
Can I quarrel with unseen forces?

But I will fight you
You that molest my creation
And make me guilty
Even when by nature I am innocent
 I won't swerve, nor bow to your shallow mockery
Neither will my eyes rain
From your shadow masked insults

The Quest

Sting me not,
Your inherent vices gave me birth
Its life precede my evolvement
I'm I now a sacrifice to redeem
Your sleazy conscience.

Answer me!
Moral monks and wood conscience
Whose iniquities are legion
Cast they first stone
If your conscience is without skeletons.

I beg you
Allow me even the dirtiest of air
I seek to walk alone even in the seventh earth
I desire no soul mate
I desire not your pleasures
I desire not your pleasantries
I desire not your pollutions
    As for your
        Divinities
        Deities
        Moralities
        Wood conscience

You can keep to yourself and your ilk's
After all I am an evil spawn
Unworthy of your tribe
    Allow me
    be
    What I am.
    That even I
    Know not.

(Dec. 2000)

**In defense of those born out of wedlock whom the society refers as bastards whereas it's the parents that gave them life that should be so called.*

Kenn Amaechi Jnr.

NOT MY SONG

I will sing the songs
That comes from my bosom
The creator created me
With an open mouth
And not a sealed tongue
You can sing what you want to sing
You can hear what you want to hear
The earth rotates in freewill.
Don't yell that am mad
Because my songs
Are not your songs
    Tell me
When it has become a sin
For one to seek his innings
The creator
Seek not my judgment
Until I stand before him
On judgment day
If they be one, the way men think.
For Gods ways are not our ways
God's thoughts not the way we do
Yet man on his own decree things
Not within his knowledge and humanity
Hangs in limitations.

Am not yet a convict
Those that are condemned
Live in jail
And those that do evil
Do so in the dark
Am a child of the light

So what is my offence?
That I accept
The creator created desire
The creator created feelings
The creator gave

The Quest

Desires and feelings expression.

Or does the devil have power of creation?
I seek to know!

Am transparent and light
Am not righteous only the creator is
I strike per second to do good.

Am confounded in this mystery
Why feed me with adrenaline and stoop my release?
Can one eat and not empty his bowels
What are the reasons for our senses?
Sure to receive and transmit
Its nature and nature
Knows best,

It's not my song
Its nature's song.

"Our fight and flight against our emotions and reactions to innate feelings are some of the mysteries humanity requires express explanations from the creator God" – Kenn Amaechi Jnr.

Kenn Amaechi Jnr.

APOCALYPSE

    At a wayside inn
    where sex is sold
    for one pound ten
    I met with my father
    My Rev. Father
    in embrace with desire
    tomorrow Saturday comes
    I will go for confession
    to confess to my father
    of our common sin
     the burden of the cross
    the cross of religion.
     The thorn to salvation
    The tears of grace.

(January 2000)

"Salvation comes through the grace of God and not the religion of Mankind" – Kenn Amaechi Jnr

The Quest

THE GOOD SHEPHERD

Today
is another Sunday
like the good sheep
we will follow the good shepherd
to hear sermon,
eat Jesus on the altar
sing, dance and chorus
    Amen, Amen, Amen

Rev. Father Xanvier is ministering
Resplendent,
radiating piously,
holier and hearty
he chattered
his mouth gaping and closing
in whispers
et cum spiritu tum
like a schizophrenic thought
like a wondering reason
the sermon fizzled out
from father xanvier stuttering tongue
and fizzled out
with the altar candlelight
in smokes
into thin air
leaving no trace
of its imprint
leaving no scent
of conviction in
our seeking minds.
Later
we marched in file
to eat
the body
and drink
the blood
sacrificed by
Father Xavier

Kenn Amaechi Jnr.

floating tongue
and flowing incantations
in file we marched
back to say thanks
and hallow the fathers
waves of blessings
like good sheep
we heeded to the solemn sign
and filed out
from the church gate
like good sheep out of the shepherd presence
to continue with the gentle sin
we left at the gate of salvation.

(2000)

**Written after observing a mass in Maiduguri said by a white reverend father whose speech was incomprehensive to the congregation.

The Quest

TELL THEM

When next they
drum into your ear
the perfection in creed
tell them, let them hear
that you too
have metamorphosed
from black to white
tell them your impurity
has purified
their tongue pasted purity
tell them, that the time
is here and now
when they too
should wear their creed
in deeds and not in words
tell them, let them know
that modesty clothes modesty
and purity is the beauty
of the pious one,
let them know
that perfection does
not hide in obscurity
but shines like
the amazing stars,
Tell them that the sacred books
said it loud
that the words need the body
and the body need the words
but first the body
must be fed and strong
to keep the word.
Tell them, a hungry man
has no appetite for pious gospel
but an appetite for pious food-pellet
tell them that you are
tired of being an opium eater
for charlatans welfare
tell them you are not

Kenn Amaechi Jnr.

a conduit for self-aggrandizement
on an empty breast plate of righteousness
Tell them you too need
The graceful bounties
To keep affluent with the spirit
tell them that we all
and not i
 have to be our brothers keepers.
Tell them, let them hear
that when you are at par
in prosperity and affluence
in lands and floating assets
in deluxe automobiles and private jets
then and only then
shall we all sing
even if on coated tongue
the sweet and beautiful
songs of tithe
        Creed
        Perfections
        and
        Purity.

"Religion indeed is the opium of the masses" – Karl Marx
"For even the son of man did not come to be served but to serve and to give his life as a ransom for many" – Mark 10:45.

The Quest

TAKE ME THERE

> Take me there
> Into the ocean of grace
> Immerse me into the waters
> Purify me
> Let me be
> Sanctified
>
> Take me there
> Into the mountains of grace
> Lift me up into the reach
> Of thine amazing presence
> Let the awesome clouds
> > Wrap me
> > In thine
> > Majesties.
>
> Take me there
> Into the depthless
> Realms of nothingness
> Let me float
> In the firmament
> Of thine gracefulness.
> John 1:17

(March 2003)

TAKE ME THERE II

Take me there
 Into the lands
 Where no iniquity dwells
 Take me there
 Into the ocean
 Where no impurities abound
 Take me there
 Into the mountains
 That lack twist and turns
 Take me there
 Into the winds
 That blow peace
 Take me there
 Into the heavens
 Where no cloud hangs
 Take me there
 Into the sanctuary
 Have sin-less-ness

 Take me there
 Into your court
 Where the verdict
  Is
   Freedom.   John 8:1-11,

(March 2003)

The Quest

TAKE ME THERE III

>Take me there
> To grace glory
> Tend me gingerly
> Touch mine spirit gently
> Tenderly bless me generously
>
>Take me there
> Thrill me in the waters
> Throw me into the oceans
> Toss me into the seas
> Teach me to swim in the river
> Let me float in faith
> Throne of your abundant grace.
> (John 7: 37-38)

(March 2003)

**God's grace is priceless, is God choosing to bless us irrespective of our selves, past, present and future. God's grace is God made pure in our life.

GIVE ME A SONG

Give me a song
  To sing your praises
  To the ears of the universe
  Of your eternal goodness
  To me, to humanity.

Give me a song to proclaim your majesty
Above the heavens
Let the earth sing of your glory
Let the people shout for joy
And let the earth
Vibrate with your holy passions

Give me a song
To feed the desires of my youths
And quench the thirst of the flesh

Give me a song
To fill the vacuum in my heart
And renew in me
The quest for your glory

Give me a song,
Give me praise,
And make me whole
In your kingdom.

(August 2005)

**Written after my Call to the bar by the Supreme Court. My ability to go to the Law School was by divine grace. Thus, my passing out and call to the bar was an amazing fulfillment.

"Give praise to God even though you are in the mouth of a lion" –
Hausa Proverbs

The Quest

I SEEK YOU

    I seek you
    because
    I love you,
    I love you
    Because
    I lost you
    I seek you
    Not for my salvation on earth
    Because
    My conception
        Birth
        Life
    And death
    You have destined.

    I seek you
    Because my heart
    Is void
    My mind, vacuumed
    And my sight
    Blind of the reason
    For my quest
    On earth
    To do good
    To make heaven.

    I seek you
    Because I want a reason
    For my travails on earth.

    I seek you
    Because
    I seek to be free
    From the chains
    Of right and wrong
    I want to be free
    From the fetters

Of ecclesiastic morality

I seek you
Because
My mind
Yearn to be loosed

I seek you
Because
my spirit
   body
   soul
seek freedom
     from
    "inhibitions"
from all passions
under your sun
in your earth.
(September 2005)

"God is all we need all the time for "if the son of God has set you free, you are free indeed" according to John 8:36" – Kenn Amaechi Jnr.

The Quest

I SEE YOU

        I see you
    In all my trials and tribulations
        I see you
    In the storm and wind
        I see you
    In the crest and trough
        I see you
    In the bricks and stones
        I see you
    In the earthquake
        I see you
    In The Windmills
        Of my life.

You have been there
From the beginning
And you have seen me through
Your gentle voice
Has called on me to be strong
Your hands has led me
Through a resting pasture
Your wholesomeness
Gave wings to my faith in you
The pillar of my being
You made me wholesome.

*Written in September 2005 after I passed my Law School exams

"When your faith is firmly built in Gods omniscience there is nothing that you cannot achieve and were as you suffers challenges in your pursuit, your faith in God will make your burden light and grant you peace even in trials. With God it's all a win win" – Kenn Amaechi Jnr

Kenn Amaechi Jnr.

LOVE TO LOVE YOU

Let the shores sing your praise
Let the oceans roar in glory
Let the seas flows in majesty
Let the mountains spread in joy
Let the earth quake in worship
to the lord our God.
I

    You stretch forth your arm
    The universe came to be
    You said let it be
    And all creatures breathed life
    Your vision is the world
    Your art is perfection.

    How do I sing a song for you ?
    How do I capture your awesomeness?
    how do I tell, the tale of my conception?
    How do I understand the mystery of my being?
    How do I comprehend the miracle of living?
    How do I understand those little things?
    That excite me about you,
    The happiness within
    At the mention of your name
            God I want to know you.

    All my life
    I want to sing your praise
    I want to hug you, till the kingdom come
    I want to rest on your bosom
    I want to breathe your goodness
    I want to work where you work
    I want to feel you all day of my life.

    All nations, all people
    Love to love you
    All nations, all people
    sings your praise
    All nations, all people

The Quest

Honour your majesty
All nations, all people
Bow to your words
All nations, all people
Seek your face
All nations, all people Glorify you
All nations, all people
Bless your name
God
I love to love you.

*Written in September 2005 after I passed my Law School exams

"If you achieve the mystery of the knowledge that nothing separate you from the love of God, you have made heaven on earth. The essence of the God in as the hope of glory is acknowledging that Gods love for us is greater than our trials and imperfection" – Kenn Amaechi Jnr

Kenn Amaechi Jnr.

TOUCH MY HEART

        come
touch my heart
feel my pause
feed my thoughts
breed my breath
hold my hands
lead my sight
dwell in my sanctuary.

        come
touch my pain
see my sorrow
hold my wounds
cloth me with compassion
fill me with your passion
encompass my soul
cloud my spirit
in the light of your vision
let me float in the firmament of your glory

        come
stay and never pass me by
let thin foot prints fit my path
let thin voices sing to my vision
let thin hands tenderly tend to me
let thin thoughts fill my heart
let the earth yield your bounties
let thine heaven pour out your wisdom
let your kingdom reign

(September 2005)

"Gods touch is the magic we aspire all our life to have, it's the touch that makes us whole and makes the nonsense makes sense" – Kenn Amaechi Jnr

The Quest

THE PERFECT CURATOR

Its your voice
When the bird sings
Its your voice
That echoes in my ears
When the trees dance
Its your magic
That I see
When the sun smiles
I see your glow
When the sun glitz at dawn
I see your shadow
At the side of a waterfall
Your presence blossoms
In the freshness of the sea
In the wind
The magic of your passion
My aphrodisiac

You see the thoughts
That fills my heart
The images
That goes before my eyes
The voice that sings to my feelings

Your love tends
The world to sleep
And in quietness
We navigate the universe.

Cuddled in your wholesomeness
Is eternity motion
Life is your tenderness
Rhymed in my consciousness
And the universe
Ruptured inside the bosom

Kenn Amaechi Jnr.

Of my ecstasy
Paradise is what I feel
Heaven knows
That the creator
Is a perfect curator

His gift of creativity
The reason for my praise
Life is beautiful
With the creator on my mind.
(September 2005)

For by him all things were created, in heaven and on earth, visible and invisible, whether thrones or dominion or rulers or authorities, all things were created through him and for him. And he is before all things, and in him all things hold together – Colossians 1:16-17

The Quest

IN AWE OF YOU

        Stones
              Sands
        Desert
        Winds
And storms
The lord will yield his increase.

            Rain
       Ocean
             Seas
       Rivers
             And streams
Cease to flow
The lord shall water his seeds.

            The sun
       moon
            stars
                    firmaments
            dims
the glory of the lord will glow.

            men
                  Birds
       Become dumb
The universe will sing the lords praise.

            And
Let the forest still,
The ocean calmed,
Let the wind freeze,
Let the earth be desolate,
The universe formless,
The lord will reign in majesty.

(August 2005)

Kenn Amaechi Jnr.

ETERNAL LOVE

    Quench my thirst
    With your desire
    Fill my lust
    With your love
    Let my heart
    Dance to your songs
    And my whole beings
    Be your dwelling place

    Let your love
    Surround me
    Like the breeze
    Of morning fresh.

    At noon
    Heat my passion
    With your glory
    Breath
    Of your blazing
            Tenderness

    At dawn
    Like dew
    The heavens illuminates
    The earth
    With your amazing splendor
    And behold
    The shining grace
    Of the almighty
    Upon us

    Unto the heaven
    Spread the hope
    And faith
    of the lords goodness.

The Quest

    The heaven glorify,
        And
        The earth proclaims
        And
    All creatures' sings
    In awe and praises
        Of
    The lords
    Eternal love.

(July 2005)

**For the 1995 graduating set of the F.C.S Government Senior Science Secondary School, Potiskum, Yobe State.

"God's love for humanity is eternal. If it is thus eternal, will God ever destroy his first love totally and render his love temporary?"
– Kenn Amaechi Jnr.

Kenn Amaechi Jnr.

LOVE

(by Damilola Mojid)

Love
Like every other word
Placed in a box by society
My teacher taught;
Love your books
My mother taught;
Love your sisters
My bank taught;
Love money
The world taught;
Love who loves you.

And I did
Yes, I did love with all my heart
I loved

I loved my sister, my brother, my best friend, the money, the hustle, the fame of hard work, the power in six digits

In my love life,
I found one lover
He said the word "love" the way I said it
But He didn't love the way I loved
His love was great;
I loved His love

Obsessed as I was
Everything good; I wanted
I went out to isolation to know of this man's love

His love was different
He lover the begger,
He loved the thief
He lover the glutton
He loved the addict

The Quest

He loved not money;
Yet wealthy
Those He loved Him not back;
Yet He loved more
He fought for them
Yet they fought Him
He died for them;
Yet they doubt Him

I love this love
I desire this love
He says I can have this love

A love that has no end
No limit, no death
All the way to the after life

I would give my all to love this way
I would follow this man
I would learn about this man
In my heart I would accept Him
His language will I speak
His grace I would boast in
Like He loves I would love

I won't rest till I am like Him
I won't stop till I can laugh with Him
Till I can cry with Him
Till I can live with Him
And Him in me

I choose this race
I choose this pursuit
Till my last breath
I would pursue.
(June 2015)

"Human life is everywhere; a state in which much is to be endured and little to be enjoyed. All the same life duty is commensurate to life beauty" – Unknown

Kenn Amaechi Jnr.

TIME FLIGHT

      Seeing through
      The thread of time
         Outstretched
         on specter
         of the heart
      In the twinkle
      of an eyelid
      gaze of millennium
      Spectrumed mind
         The moon
      becomes our resting place
         The sun
      becomes our warming rays
         The earth
      becomes our footpath
      the stars cheers and claps
         Over
      our conquered universe
         leaving behind
      footprints
      on the sands of time.

(June 1998)

"He who masters his time masters his life" – Mike Murdock

The Quest

TIME MESSAGE

    We talk much
    Meaning less
    In our wide wild tales
    we are alike
    with kings and queens
    The sky is not our limit
    but
        The stretch of mid-noon
        And wee-night dream songs
        Dreamt into the
        sea of fantastic oblivion
        creating ideal world
        for ideal life
        in our ideal dream

    We ain't alone
    In this shallow journey
    We have seen too
    The descent steps
    of failure and frustration
    on the faces
    of our once role models
    whose dreams of footprints
    on the sands of time
    have been achieved
    on their white hairs
    sneezing snuff nose
    and eccentric tempers

    Our journey is on
    A familiar terrain,
    Though, if we have choice
    We'd choose to have
    a compass and direct
    The point of our dream
    Our destiny determined.

Kenn Amaechi Jnr.

We follow
the crowd without the crown
In this fountain of utopia
achieved but unreached
felt but untouched
seen but unknown.

Come Obi,
Count our milestones
Isa, follow our wrinkles
And tell us its memories
Perhaps we have grown
old in our dreams.

We have been up from time set
And doeth nothing
For time has stolen
Our days and dreams
For no goals seems
to be reached
And nothing be pursued.

Now!
we have grown doubly wise
In our shrinking coat
And rumpled agbada
The glittering silver
In our hairs
Tells us to dream less
Talk less
Our talk and dreams
have become
A relic
of scattered visions.

(June 1998)

"Dreams are not fortune neither hope on asset they can wither and die" – Unknown

The Quest

TWILIGHT

They have learned all there is to learn
They have won the Crown of Science and Art
They have mastered the universe
The heart of men their draught board

They had gazed at space in roaring silence
With hollow blinkless eyes
    In their quest
    They have drunk to stupor
    The tonic
    of pen
       paper
          Relived
              the un-lived
          of theorists,
            inventors
          and formulators

What they come to learn
They have learned
What they come to change
They have changed
What they come to search
They have found
What they dreamt
They have seen at half past
What they come to achieve
They have achieved
        All
        All of them
        In their embattled
        White hair and bald heads.

(June 1998)

"Professors in the universities are delight to behold, but their living standard is not commensurate to their gifts to humanity" – Kenn Ameachi Jnr.

Kenn Amaechi Jnr.

NATURE

      Nature
      Nurtured naught
      Naught nurtured humanity
      to fight with
      Nature Nurtures.
      Man wrestled with force
      And got knocked out
      of living
      into
           existing
           in imbalance.   (Dec 2002)

"God doesn't play dice, or does he?" – Albert Einstein

NIGHT II

>Night
> Your wiles and warmth
> Confound me
> Under your shadow
> Evil is hatched
> And many breath
> Ceased to breath.
> Under your shadow
> God's omnipotence manifests
> And the hands
> Of the almighty
> In infinite love
> Perfects the art of creation
> Night
> Though you scare
> Your breath breezes
> Virgin   strength
> Virgin dream
> Virgin hope
> Virgin idea
> To life lives
> As the amazing glory
> Of the almighty
>   Might
>   Over
>   Nature's night.

(July 2004)

Kenn Amaechi Jnr.

BIRTH TO DEATH

>In the order
>of birth to death
>faith and fate
>father and mother
>will depart un-accosted
>to the abyss of slurred memories
>in the stream mind
>of sons and daughters'
>who will follow
>the flow into
>the realms of oblivion
>and beneath the bush path
>a white grave house
>where our clan
>shall dwell
>each to himself
>All for God
>till the
>>Kingdom
>>Comes.

(May2001)

"Death is the privilege of human nature, life without it is not worth living" – Unknown

The Quest

RICHES IN LIMBO

Chief Otokoto
is wealthy, he is rich
A Chief, a titled man
A Knight, a philanthropist
A man of many means
    But
Chief Otokoto
walks on lonely pathways
treks on pathetic sideways
talks with ghosts, sleeps open-eyed
Lives in lonely darkness
groping in the cloud
of yesterday's evil.

Chief Otokoto
slaughtered his kith and kin
cut his own genealogy
for money rituals.

Chief Otokoto
lives a lifeless life
walking with ghosts
walking in darkness
walking in clouds.
life without light
light without rays
rays without radiance
Radiance without glow
glow without sunshine
    Chief Otokoto
    is a walking
    wealth in limbo.

(August 2002)

"Better to be poor than to be rich and wretched in soul" –
Unknown

Kenn Amaechi Jnr.

BLISS OF PARADISE

        I have thought
        thoughtlessly into
        thoughtlessness
        I have dreamed
        dreamlessly into
        dreamlessness
        which begets
        yet more
        thoughts and dreams
        I have gazed widely
        Out of imaginations
        Fantasy has brought
        diamonds
            golds
            silvers
        On my doorsteps
        I had lived
        lived like King Solomon
        in opulence & splendor
        while lying on my bed
        with eyes
        outstretched
        gazing penetratingly
        into
            the
                bliss of paradise
        with my dream lenses
            (November 1998)

"Without dreamers mankind would still be living in caves" –
Anable France

The Quest

DEATH OF AN EMPIRE

>Herein
>Lies in limbo
>Blind
>>Unfeeling
>>Numb
>
>A would be mineral resource
>A decaying treasure
>of acidified earth
>Dr. Chief Omego
>Who while he breathed,
>was CEO, founder
>Chairman, President
>
>He transverse
>depth and beyond
>those that were less fortunate
>to him are parasites
>losers and undesirables.
>He lived in self-made eldorados
>But he died
>Was mourned
>by self
>in a lonely paradise
>filled with earthworms
>himself an *unhistory*
>of grave relic
>for those that
>look back
>at infamy.

(February 2000)

"Greed is the sole element that has kept humanity in chaos since time immemorial" – Unknown

Kenn Amaechi Jnr.

MY HERO

    Your hands
    You laid on me
    your right hand
    you have laid on me
    taking me
    through the lonely path
    even to the valley of loneliness
    friends asks?
    If all is well?
    For you made me too humble
    painted me blue
    thereby forcing me to retreat
    From the multitude
    as the blue sky
    Times before now
    I wished
    I were different
    But not any more
    For you have opened
    My eyes
    Making me
    to see reason,
    the reason
    for my being

HAPPINESS IN CREATIVITY

(for Sam Alahiya and all lovers of creativity)

>
> Now I stand before my creator
> My creator
> I praise above all.
>
> My talent
> I will sing of you
> to all the living
> for you were with me
> through
>   thick
>   thin
>   and tears
> giving me songs in the darkest night
> you truly never let me go lonely
> for even hardship
> you have painted aesthetically
> giving me companions
> even through hell
>
> Now I pray you
> Inhabit the world
> make your home
> in the heart of men
> keeping him
> from the wiles
> of the wicked
> even the destructive
> of anger and provocations
> for these cannot dwell with you
> my talent
> you are
> my hero.

(June 2001)
"Art is nothing more than the shadow of humanity" – *Henry James*

I WEPT

I wept
In the shadow of Irony
Under the strength of weakness
With the heart of water melon
The hope of hopelessness
The search for nothingness
The grope into darkness
The valiancy of cowardice
The sight of blurred vision
I wept.

I wept
And ask
Where and when
Did I wrong right
      Was it?

In the pursuance of knowledge
In the thirst for fulfillment
In the leap to catch my dream
In the believe to touch the sky
In the search for hazy visions
In the yearning to appease disgruntled mind
In the desire to kiss justice.

My thoughts run wide
Like the scattering of smoke
Hands stretched to have a feel
Of the reason
Then comes the flow of epileptic pangs
I wept.

I wept
Now, can tell
The twist of fate
The hypocrisy of destiny
The prostitution of ambition

The Quest

      The whoring of dream at mid day
      The deceit of believe
      The blindness of vision
      The inertia of prowess
      The emptiness of reality
The betrayal of ancestors

    I wept

    I wept
    Tears, gathered
    A garlant of rivers
    Encircling the root
    Of my up-turned canoe
    To nourish and strengthen
    Decaying soul and numb stumps
    Of my decaying dream roots
    I wept.

    I wept
    Into the tide of time
    I reminisced
    To see my scattered self
    In the destructive wind
    Of misfortune
    I wept

    To the stars
    I take flight
    To reach my
    Silver linings
    And conquer
    The world
    Of my childhood dream
     I wept:

**Written in 1997 after I was offered History as a course of study in the University Of Maiduguri against my desire to read Law.

Kenn Amaechi Jnr.

I LEARN WITH TEARS

I learn with tears
Regretful tears
Bearing of ambition lost
A cloud darkens its skyline
My search turned to naught

I learn with tears
Regretful tears
Cradle to study the statutes
Justice and equity
My burning destinations
Alas!
Nepotism and sectionalism
Impelled.

I learn with tears
Regretful tears
Intervening circumstances
Draw me backward
To great-grandfather's ages
Dark ages of stone and iron
Dark ages of crafted gods

I learn with tears
Regretful tears
Past shadow of ape-man
Old traditions, old customs
Of slaves, slavery and slave masters
Of colonies, colonialism and colonial masters
Of independence struggle and nationalism
Of development and developing calabash
Of tripolar, bipolar and unipolar calabash
Of wars, conquest and kingdom
Of ancients and civilizations
I was compelled
To mirror watch

The Quest

I learn with tears
Regretful tears
Mind transmuted to the past
To look backward and
Recreate forward
With termite search
For historical antecedents

ow knowing past
Could create future
I gazed to know.

I learn with tears
Regretful tears
Friends say
It's repulsive
Kith and kin
Frown derisively
Society terms it
Backward drive
To backlashes
The academic assures
That all knowledge is wealth.

I stood in a maze
To watch the twist
Of fate
The fate of destiny
The destiny of History.

(March 1997)

**Written after my admission to study History when I actually applied and qualified to study law at the University of Maiduguri

Kenn Amaechi Jnr.

POCKET YOUR ANGER

I can see the fire of adolescent
Burning in your eyes and tongue
but I am afraid
the heat of that fiery fire
may consume the fine flesh in you
and make garbage of all that
gallantry feats you aim to reach
so pocket your anger.

We too also wrestled with force
but never won the battle
we got wickedly bruised
by heartless thorns of tradition
which have chained us
to its ugly infirmities
though we have know all the wisdoms
we can't break the shackle of customs.

It's this tradition
that allows the old man slap you
when you tell him the truth
that imprisons your tongue
to the absurdities of man's meanness
that wrong your right intensions
that hanged your emotions
to your throat
binds you to an unwholesome marriage
that keeps you in bondage to servitude

pocket your anger
you aren't the only one
that carries the yoke and cross
of it's oppressive burdens.
 Generation past also bore the burden to their grave
 We struggled with tradition's iniquities
 but our morale got soaked
 in the feces of tradition.
 We went and bowed to it's prerogatives

The Quest

    and picked up the remains of our
    battered self
        Carpentered
        painted
        and straightened.

"I think tradition is the prerogative of fools. Things should be seen and accepted on their merit to current realities and not based on some archaic traditions that subjugate others to its banalities" – Kenn Amaechi Jnr

Kenn Amaechi Jnr.

AIDS

Acquired at the honey pot of humanity
Immune to grave sorrow and agony
Deficient to man's concocted galaxy of remedies
Syndrome of a near extinct degenerate
generation

Your birthday, a death day
Our death day
Our song now is gone too soon
To the lewd call of vain pleasure -
Painlessly we mourn
A painful death

Your venom spares not the innocent
embryo the mother's womb
You inflict with your killjoy virus
Carried from the placenta
Of a sacrilegious womb
Condemned by a putrid
Flight of cursed senile.

Into your grave
Goes the gorgeous
Shrunk cadaver
Of a once excellent creature
Hanged by a perfect creator
For a moral wrong
Born out of moral void
In a world
    Of
Amoral deities.

(July 2002)

"Aids is fast becoming the biggest threat to humanity after hunger, our world, our life, can be safer if we stoop to conquer our inanity and love ourselves more than lust" – Ken Amaechi Jnr.

The Quest

BEAST OF EXTINCTION

    In the garden of vice
      Humanity veered into
      Vulnerable casual callousness
      And got visited
      By bands of bawdy song-stress
      With lewd sense
      Of human essence.
      Humanity was aided
      To swim in the murky waters
      Of natures impulsive desires
      And assuage the burning flame
      Of a body of auto-magnetic attraction
      We slumped into lascivious lust
      That begot an infectious monster.
      Humanity was blessed
      With the yoke of sin
      The donation
      A doomed gene of death
     The beast of extinction!
      Born at the vineyard
      Of Eden's garden of vice
      Extinction of God's famous creation
      Though
      We await heaven panacea
      And science benevolence
      For a remedy
      We remain
      Blind to the genesis
      Of a viral revelations.

(November 2002)

"A number of us live life because life is life and we have to live. But let's live life because we have future dreams, let's live based on a mission and a vision of living... So let's hold hands and fight against HIV/AIDS we can make it..." – Nelao, 21-year-old HIV positive Namibian

Kenn Amaechi Jnr.

CARO

Caro
is a trader
but not in the market place
nor in street shops
She is a hawker
but not of
palmwine
    nor *ogiri*
neither *tuwo*

Caro's
trade is on the mat
She has her goods
embedded inside
the creators benevolent
gift of procreation
Her shop can be found
in the bosom laying place
of Chief *Okoro*
    Otunba Owolabi
    Alhaji Maikudi
and Mr. *Spoke ride*
whose milky poking
stick has no conscience.

Caro is not
the only merchant
in the trade
her compatriots
are like weeds
growing and sprouting
from depraved queens
of our jungle society.

    Caro,
her colleagues, and customers
Are deaf and blind to the violent fire
That consumes hawkers of the red holes

The Quest

        and porous sticks and stifle their body
        Into a ghost of walking skeletons
         If they know what that simmering touch
        Can cause they would have hidden under the
        Nylon shield.
Alas!
        the long virus is eager to go violent into
        Stubborn pits.

(September 2002)

Kenn Amaechi Jnr.

NKOSI JOHNSON

The gods condemned you
before your creation
that gave you a lifeless existence
into a contemptible world

Your childhood innocence
A phenomenal revelations
Of holy cruelties sanctified by the gods
That revel at infanticide

Your steel strength
Your grand courage
To live amidst condemnation
Enkindled the heart of the faithful
In a faithless condition.

Your clarion call
To the world
A sparkling rose
That gingered ugly souls
Of an apathetic world
Into a new awakening.

You whispered to soul mates in pain
That you have a home in heaven
You were a grace
That shone out compassion
And kindled the light
for a brighter
Healthier tomorrow.

(November 2002)

***Nkosi Johnson a South African, was born with AIDS. He died of AIDS at the age of twelve. While he lived, he preached for love and not hate for those living with HIV/AIDS.*

The Quest

CHAOS CITY (I)

    The sun was hot
      The breeze hot
      We bathed in perspiration
      As we hastened to bye
      The *Shehu's* scorching but calm city
      To a paradise in *Oba's* Garden
    We were heavy
      With pleasant expectations
      Of a smiling warm city
      With spontaneous charisma
      And arms spread in amiable embrace
      To natures serenity
      Tranquility our expected
      Gate keeper
          Alas!
      We were hit by a thunderbolt of chaos
      In the city of excellence
      Confusion, commotion, collusion
      Bid us welcome
      We had a concussion
      And got punctured
      In the belly
      To a premature delivery
      Of a constipated pregnancy
      Squirmed in dejavu
      Of prodigal remembrance
      Of the serenity
      Of the land of peace.

(August 2002)

***My immediate impression of Lagos State, on my first visit in 2002. I passed through Oshodi and it was like swarming in a murky heat wave of chaos.*

"Lagos is a magical city it entices one with its thrills and frills and saps you out before you exhale" – Kenn Amaechi Jnr.

CHAOS CITY (II)

    Chaos city
    Is spread
    Like a conundrum of commotion
    A centrifugal force of confusion
    Centripetally located for collusion of men
    Of traffic
    Of garbage
    Of miscreant and misfits
    Of religious abracadabra
    Of politricks
    Of dirty tricks
    Of social razzmatazz
    Entangled in a fisticuff
    Of fittest survival
    Eko stands
    Wizardly embroiled in chaos
  Weirdly wired to junk life
    Romantically enthralling
    Passionately enticing
    Eko stands
  Defiantly menacing
    Brazenly compelling
    Brightly alluring

    Eko city
  Like the lagoon
  Is a confluence?
    Of social convolution.

(August 2002)

**My immediate impression of Lagos State, on my first visit.

The Quest

OSHODI

Oshodi!
Oshodi-Oke
Where men, mic and ghosts tread

Oshodi
A maze of bizarre scenes
Of our frightful circumstances
Where all men are goats
Driven by impulsive instincts
To burn out the oil of life
To quench the flame of living
For another life to be lived
In a ghost-land paradise.

Oshodi
Where automobiles and men
Are victims and offenders?
Of auto magnetic traffic jam.
Where heads are stalls and tarmacs makeshifts shops
Men and *molues f*ight for right of way
In an amphitheatre of commotion.

Oshodi
The homestead
Of our world trade centre

Oshodi
Markets all marketable
Junks and junkites
With *Oshodi* to poetic sound that draws
Our pleasant and appalling patronage.

(August 2002)

**My immediate impression of Oshodi, Lagos State, on my first visit as it was before Raji Fashola cleansed the mess.

Kenn Amaechi Jnr.

BURNING FLAME

        Set my candle alight
        With kisses that burn my lips
        Touch my precious secrets
        Fetch my mountain juice
        Wrap me in
        Ecstatic clouds
            Heaven
            Our climax.

(January 2002)

        (For you, yes you)

"We can't do without love is that scent of attraction toward others which makes us more humane and alive; it's simply the earth in passionate motion"

The Quest

EVERGREEN

for Anthonia Ibeson *(as she then was)*

        Your love blossoms
        In my heart
        It burns me into reality
        It makes me glitter
        It illuminates my globe
        It brightens my vision
        Of how much
                I love you

        Your love
        Bleaches away
        the scars of the past
        it nurtures a blissful future
        It tickles me alive
        As it grows
        Heavier
        Each day.

        Your love
        Has a special touch
        In my system
            My sanctuary
        Where it grows
            greater
            Even greener   for my mama
                Forever.

(November 2000)

"Love is the strongest tide in the sea of life, it moves mountain, it crosses bridges, it transverses ocean, it survives even death" – *Anonymous*

Kenn Amaechi Jnr.

FARE WELL TO MAMA

........But............
Did you ever live?
 Your flame was brief
In between youth and when you found love
And perhaps those times you birthed to life
.....Us....your children.

Did you ever live?
When the tempest set in
With your soul, you fought
And clinched to a love long lost
And eternally denied your self
The grace to live.

Sorrow was given an open door
And with each passing
A breeze of pain and mirage
Of life.

I deeply wish with all my being
And with an earnest craving
As my heart beats, that you
Find life and live in eternal peace with our God.

R.I.P. Dear mother...
We will always love you!!!

The Quest

THE PRECIPICE

        Love
That which turn men
Deaf and dumb
And twists their hearts
Into emotional battles fields
        Seeing but not conceiving
        Hearing but not perceiving
        Feeling but not accepting

The earth turns round
Like wheel on cycle
Revolving stricken hearts
To its breaking precipice
        But so it was made to be
        From divine creations
        That all kinds be bound in love
Amidst the crest and trough
Of inhibiting phobias

Bird sings sonorously, lovingly
Lakes and streams flow in romantic passion
Rivers and ocean roars in erotic embrace
Cloud and sky rumble in roaring ecstasy
Beasts of the jungle
Whine in happy fantasy
None is lonely
In this quest for
A mystic feel
That earthquake
The earth's equation
Into a climatic
        Precipice

(January 2002)

"Gravity cannot be held responsible for people fallen in love" –
Albert Einstein.

Kenn Amaechi Jnr.

SILENT WISHES

(for Amaka Anaza - a love made in diaspora)

If silence were worlds
If silence is to speak
The word isn't enough
To echo out the sound of my silence

If heart beat can be heard
My chest a heart dance
To the mystic rhythm
Of your glowing heart strings

If feelings can be seen
I will fly like the butterfly
Cascading radiant colours
Into the sky
And spread my feelings
In shed of violet
For the world to see
my feelings for you

if dreams were for sale
I will buy for myself
      You
To keep forever.

(August 2005)

The Quest

FRAGRANCE OF LOVE

    The fragrance of love is in the air
    The sons and daughters of cupid
    Breath in the freshness of dew
    Flowing like a river
        In the hearts
        Of heartthrobs

    The fragrance of love is in the air
        Sweet songs echoes
        From heaven
    The rhythms
    Of love birds and the sky
    Clothed in passionate splendour
    Spreads warmth of tender beauty on the earth
    Like the sixth day of creation
    A stream of love flowed
        in cuddled embrace
    and watered
        the gardens of Eden.

The fragrance of love is in the air
    A fountain
    From the oasis of love.

    Open your heart
    And let your feelings
    flow like a river
    into the sea
    of boundless ecstasy.

    Look into my eyes
    And never let go
    The springs of paradise
    Found and free.
**One Valentine day that was truly red, February 14, 2010

Kenn Amaechi Jnr.

THE MOMENT I BEHELD THEE

The moment I beheld thee
The world melted
The universe vaporised
The earth stilled
All songs ceased to sing

Nothing seems to be
          But
Your aura of love
My heart is pierced
My souls take a flight
To the wonderland of never land.

For your heart
I will soar
Like the eagle
To reach the sky
And paint our love
In beautiful colours
Of the rainbow
The stars will gaze in awe
And dance to our glory.

I will fly
Into the heavens
To proclaim my princess
Before the highest priest
And let the angels
Be my witness
For a love eternal.

(September 2005)

The Quest

NIGHT

    Night
       You crept in
       In ominous silence
       Awestruck in thy serene calm
       My adventurous reverie confined
       To the shelter of a walled home
       Where I must seek refuge
       At the sight
       Of your deep dark beauty
       Though you entrap me
       With a danger unknown.
       Which you swears hide
       Under the burrow of darkness
       With cudgels and catapult
       To lay siege on me
       You turn to my sensuous senses
       With passionate caress
       Endearing me to the warmth
       Embrace of a heartthrob
       As cupid beckons
       To cover us
       With a romantic shield
       And the designs
       Of the creator
       Perfect itself in a
    Freewill omnipotence.

(July 2004)

Kenn Amaechi Jnr.

Childhood is the all exciting scene in the theatre of a tragic-comic life tale that we often wish the beginning does not exeunt and the end is suspended, it is sunset that black out at dawn.

The Quest

SHADOWS

It is not
A late understanding
I had borne
The cross
From crawlers-age
Though I never slept
Over the difference.
Now that my height
Has grown with my reasoning
Scale of the imbalance
Explodes my quiet
Resignation.

The ascendancy shadows
Of a depraved childhood
Obfuscate the blissful
Excitement of happy remembrance,
    The bliss
Of adolescent eccentrics.

The touch of affection
From the springs of effervescent innocence
Have left a heart bleeding
Out of a broken wall
Of memories of agony
Years of neglect
Vacuum of deprived love
Is flashing back to me
Like a wave of hot breeze
The impact weighing
Me down
    At dawn
    Deep
Memories of broken innocence.

My hands are
    outstretched
    search-groping

Kenn Amaechi Jnr.

    for
my childhood laughters
smiles of contentment
Boyish shyness for favour
 long
long
distance
of unknown existence
 perhaps
 from
mashed
innocence.

(November 1999)

The Quest

SONG FOR MYSELF

I am a fine boy
I have no pimples
I have dimples
which make me laugh
when virtually I lack.

I am a have-not
In the midst of the haves
I live but a life of faith
To have a temporary feel
of that thing that makes
the faces of the haves
glitters.

My face
Also glitters
not from accumulated reservoirs
of fats
     proteins
       and oils
but from a religious message
of bath
     cheerfulness
       and happiness
Sleep too, is a luxury
My wholesale thoughts
stretch as long
as the length
of a daily bread
And as short
as the size
of bend-down rags
to cover
my priceless
    body.

They that have

Kenn Amaechi Jnr.

> I grudge not
> For tomorrow too
> I will be king
> If not here
> Certainly in the
> Firmament above.

(November 1998)

"Life can be fun when nothing; I mean nothing, really matters except living by the grace of tomorrow's fortune" – Kenn Amaechi Jnr.

The Quest

REMINISCENCES

My river flows into sea
Yet the sea is not filled
My stream runs inside the depth
Yet it has no end
Slow passionate flows
Of my sweet childhood blues.

My heart flow too
With the rhythms of my dream stream
Body and soul carried away
To sky height of ecstasy
The memories of sweet childhood blues.

I feel I can fly
Wings spread towards
The heavens
To catch up with hazy visions
Of sweet memories
Of my childhood blues.

I heard the resonant flow calling
I dream and reminisce
Days of naked innocence
Of paradise on earth
Dreams of sweet childhood blues.

Dreams
Of castles and palace
Of heroic deeds and conquest
Of tender love and happy days
All bright and beautiful
In the eyes and visions
Of sweet childhood blues.

Dreams
Of world bereft
Of pain, sorrow and fear

Kenn Amaechi Jnr.

The triple-horned evils
That darken age of reality
And turn our dreams
Into fragments of broken calabash
Breaking the breezy wave
of sweet childhood blues.
(February 2000)

Is there anything as amazing as childhood?

The Quest

WHEN I WAS A CHILD

When I was a child
Child child child
I thought like a child
Child child child
I played like a child
Child child child

I laughed like a child
Child child child
I cried like a child
Child child child

When I was a child
Child child child
I lived like a child
I lived like a child
A life full of peace
A life full of joy
A life full of love
A life full of happiness
When I was a child
Child child child.

(December 2002)

Kenn Amaechi Jnr.

I WANT TO HEAR A LULLABY

I want to hear a lullaby
Lullaby lullaby
When my eyes rain a tear
Lullaby lullaby
I want to hear a lullaby
Lullaby lullaby
When mummy is away
Lullaby lullaby
When daddy is away
Lullaby lullaby
When angel is away
Lullaby lullaby
I want to hear a lullaby
Lullaby lullaby
When the wind raises a dust
Lullaby lullaby
When the earth shakes a quake
Lullaby lullaby
When the rain fells a home
Lullaby lullaby
When the heavens gather a cloud
Lullaby lullaby
I want to hear a lullaby
Lullaby lullaby
When peace falls apart
Lullaby lullaby
When reason is shattered
Lullaby lullaby
When war song are sung
Lullaby lullaby
When the world goes crazy
Lullaby lullaby
When the world becomes lonely
Lullaby lullaby
I want to hear a lullaby
Lullaby lullaby.

The Quest

CHILDHOOD PARADISE

Childhood was paradise
Playing hide and seek
Under the udara tree
And inside mama's Butterfly wrapper
Wrapped in the peace of innocence
Without the wisdom of faith
All fears and dreams
Were cast upon
The sands of the earth
The tickle of the clock
Never meant a thing
And time pursued us
To mature and inherits
The incurable ailment
Of mankind,
        Pride and prejudice

Childhood was heaven
Bathing with the sands
And swimming in the rain
Breathing, inhaling
All the passions and magic
Of creation
The cloud was a cloudy distraction
The rainbow a beautiful amazement
The moon and the stars
A gracious glowing companion
Inside the cloud called heaven
God, Jesus and the angels dwell
And there was no greed
No passion for evil.
God was never a punisher
And Jesus loved us
The angels guard while we sleep
The church was beautiful
With beautiful clothes and songs
A Naira for the reverend
Every body goes home happy

Kenn Amaechi Jnr.

No condemnation no penance
Hell fire exist not

Childhood was bliss
The world was a big brotherhood
For Christ and for Muhammad
For mary and for maryam

Childhood was bliss
A merry go round
That was
Slaughtered
    At
    Age sixteen

(September 2005)

"Let the children come to me and do not hinder them, for the kingdom of heaven belongs to such as these" – Jesus (Mathew 19: 14)

Let every soul look unto the morrow for the deed it has performed.

– Prophet Muhammed (S.A.W)

Kenn Amaechi Jnr.

HISTORIANS

    Seers
    They are
        Searching for
    Past tenants of the earth
    Remnants
    of stone ages
    Iron ages
    Dark ages
        Trans Sahara
            Trans Atlantic
                Trans Air
    They look backward
    to see forward
    The guardians of old traditions
    In the desert menaced brush of humanity
    To cleanse and purify
    the sins of yester-years
    to patch and repaint
    the potholes of our world
    To rise like the sun of creation
    and light the face of the earth
    with peace and hope
    lost commodities of today's age

    The land needs the seer
    to revive its past glory
    and raise itself
    to new heights

    The Law needs the Seer
    to tell the tale of her upbringing
    the tech and nologists need the seer
    to techno tell her evolvement
    the scientist needs the seer
    to synthesise her infancy
    the economist needs the seer
    to tell the tale of her master
    of misery

The Quest

as the roots needs the soil
for depth and steady growth
so the land needs the seer
to hold the pillar of her faculties
Listen to
the voice of the visioners
The chorus of resistant calls
To excoriate the land
of its scurvy conscience

    It is the architectural cornerstone
    The mother of all disciplines
    Invoking the past
    for beautiful future.

(March 1998)

**For my lecturers at the History Department, University of Maiduguri and all Historians. I appreciate the knowledge acquired.

Kenn Amaechi Jnr.

ADIEU HISTORIANS

We were toddlers that
crawled into giant maturity
through the forged
of intellectual and ideological
flames
of
Muktar
Waziri
Garba
Musa
Saliba
Babagana
Maimuna
Diram
Kyari

Our journey to maturity is spiritual
but you all know
life is a dual carriage way
each person to his own gate
where we must split
into parallel gateways
Here
we must pause and reminisce
on the bounds shared.
the bridge crossed together

How
Do I sing the song
of the ideas
    the principles
    the philosophies
cherished,
the smiles that broaden into laughters
which we shall leave behind
the academic conquest

the engaging peace and serenity

The Quest

>   the crest and trough
>   we passed through
>   Goodbye
>   becomes
>   A sea of memories
>   Unbreakable
>   A torrent of speeches
>   Unspoken
>   Handshakes
>   aint enough
>   to break
>   the waves
>   of emotions which soar
>   in our historic minds
>   But then
>   we are leaders
>   of men
>   we subject ourselves
>   to objective appraisals
>   crossing over
>   without blemishes
>   the hurdles of life.
>   You have left
>   But not gone
>   Ours is a sendforth
>   not send-off
>   so it's refreshingly hopeful
>   that we will
>   converge again
>   At the virgin land
>   of intellectual camaraderie
>   it's hard to say goodbye
>   Yet, I must wish you All
>   An affectionate
>   Farewell
>   Adieu.

(December 2000)
**For my course mates at the History department of the University of Maiduguri.

Kenn Amaechi Jnr.

SUNSET

I searched for song
Amongst the pathetic pathways
We treaded together
The thorny terrain
We transversed together
I searched for song
through the crest and trough
of our trek to destiny

I searched for song
In the logical conclusions
We couldn't reach
The reasonable doubts
We couldn't douse
In the dreams that drizzle despair
I searched for songs amongst the sonorous
Songsters of the night
Under the Sahara sun
In the suffocating congestions
In the chilling harmatan

I searched for song
In this bliss, this blaze
I searched for songs
Amongst the laughter's and smiles
So effervescent, so transient

Our song is sweet and sour

    But
In the colours of the rainbow
I will paint our travails
Like stars pasted in heaven
I will splash the memories shared
In golden tunes
I will sing of our trials and triumph

The Quest

Our song is sweet and sour
Our eyes are dewy, our tears is rain
Our promise is dear, our harvest is rich

Dear friends, learning colleagues
the sun is set
Our night is light
The stars and the sky is our dream
Our destiny beckons

Our song is sweet and sour
Our promise is dear
Our harvest is rich
Goodbye is rain
in the cloud of emotions
farewell into the horizon of hope
Gods providence is peace
Good luck I bid you.

**For the January 2003 graduating students of the Faculty of Law, University of Maiduguri (my course mates)

Kenn Amaechi Jnr.

AMIN AL-MUMINI

The sun rises
And sets at its peak
At noon, it has no hiding place
Except the moon eclipse
When the moon is full
Children tell tales by moonlight
Of its amazing glory
The stars colour the sky
The king star never dims
      But shines
The ending of the day
Manifests in the morning
the day done at night
the breath is foul and fresh.

When we hear a good song
We all know how to melt
To its melody.

I know not how to sing
To a deaf and dumb audience
But when the audience
Claps and cheers
Even the deaf and the dumb
Acknowledge and applause
But no one, no audience
Behold a grand actor
And live without a smile

We all know how to clip
      Our tongues
When pain and despair
Dwell I the land

The Quest

And ancient tradition echoes
Lanterns are not hidden under a bushel
And where there is light
The people find their way
We also know of good breeds
Do not blow their trumpets
And richly laden vessels
Sails gentle but gallantly

Our song is sound
Our chorus is cheers
Our song leader is marvellous
Our tongue leap for a song
    For
A quintessential performer
Gentle but great achievers
A teacher of teachers
A personification of a new dawn
The dawn of our excellence
    the excellence
    of an
    amin-al mumini

(January 2004)

**For Professor J.D Amin, former Vice Chancellor of the University of Maiduguri

AKACHI

I woke up today
My hopes told me
It's a fountain of favour
In bounteous expectation
I stepped out
To conquer the world
with my best courtesy
I beheld Akachi
The Amazon of literary exploit
The paragon of feminism
The grace of young authors
    Akachi
The kingress of letters
In a majestic humility
    Akachi
Was warm
    nice
      airless
Akachi
Was gracefully beautiful
I wanted to toast her
But then Akachi spoke
In majestic prowess
I bowed in admiration
Akachi is a queen

Akachi read my poems
And poured hibernation of commendation
Akachi said
I am great
I have potentials
    But
How do I get published?
I asked.
Akachi lost gait
And said
You have to gather courage

The Quest

And publish it yourself
Because publishers cant publish
Without money
So sorry
Literary publication is pathetic

                   2003-date.

Akachi wept for me
Such a young poet
With great lines
Sure you are encouraged
Thank you Akachi
My eyes drizzling tears
I saw the door
Looked back
The grace, the victory
Was Akashi"s rich handshake
      But
My hopes, dreams
Closed with the door
Of Akachi"s
Head of department office.

(October 2005)

**For Akachi Ezeigbo Adimora, Winner of 2002 NLNG literary prize

Kenn Amaechi Jnr.

SERVICE TO THE FATHER LAND

    Attention!!!
Identify your self
Which school are you from?
Which cult do you belong to ?
    None
Otondo....hmmmm
Run, run with your bag to the field.
Service to the father land

    Whistles
Songs, soldiers, man o war
Otondo wake up!!!
Sleep, murdered at prime
Morning menaced and undone
You are still sleeping, you are wrong
Iron beds quaking
Boots, white and sore faces
Service to the father land

Food for thought, meditations
The morality and wisdom of a uniformed commandant
Poured like libation on the heads of childhood
Meditates, pray and think great of the father land
Service to the father land.

Attention!!!
Forward match In threes
Walk, run , fly
Thrill,frills
How many girlfriends soldiers go get oooh
Them go give them HIV......
How many soldiers corpers go kill ooooh
Oooh them go kill them tire
Everybody jankara marketer
Kaduna, kaduna why you no go zamfara
Service to the fatherland

Ewedu

The Quest

Amala
Bread and beans
Watered tea
Eat, drink and don't quench
Service to the father land
Whistles
Sun, heat, endurance trek
Bush paths
Commotion
Stolen romance
Service to the father land

Songs, dance, fire light, fire love
And the beautiful ones
Radiantly entrapping
Service to the father land

Parade
Remove head dress, salutes
Youths obey the clarion call
Service to the father land

Clearance, posting
Delusions and disappointment
Service to the father land

Family house
Filthy rooms
Primary assignment
Wage less jobs
Deferred hopes
Our eyes opened
Now your suffering continues… (NYSC)
Service to the fatherland
(11TH June 2006)

**For all National Youth Service Corps members who diligently served the father land under the sun and in the rain. Bravo!!!

Kenn Amaechi Jnr.

THE LIVING SPRING

(For the peace loving people of Osun State)

Breathe in the fountain of spring
Exhale the effervescent of dawn
Flow in the spring of warmth
Live on the splendor of serenity
Dwell in the paradise of peace
Walk on the tapestry of freshness
And behold
A new Eden land
Sprawled with the flamboyance of grandeur
Clothed with the garment of nature
Fortified with the shield of pasture adorned with ornamental green
Scented with the fragrance of love

The living spring
So alluring and charming
Like a piece of paradise
Dropped from the window of heaven

The living spring
The homestead of Oduduwa
The cradle of humanity
The alter of Sango

The living spring
A land of aquatic splendor
A land of nubile beauties
A land of grail wisdom
A land of youth & vigor

The living spring
The land that my service beckons
To message the pride of the fatherland
And lift the nation higher
Under the sun
In the rain

The Quest

The living spring
A land whose benevolence
Is charming like
The kiss of love in the dew

**Written in January 2007 after passing out from the national youth service in Osogbo, Osun State.

Kenn Amaechi Jnr.

EXPECT GREAT THINGS

Expect great things
When your words are your bond
When your honor is your market value
When intergrity is your brand name
When your wisdom is caste in marbles
When your business is built on fidelity

Expect great things
When you don't wink at weird deals
When your partners are not plaited with deceit
When your books are not crooked with conked cookies
When your trade is not trailed in zig- zags
When your business is not bent with the buzz

Expect great things
When your wealth is nurtured from the cradle
When your treat is that of kings
When your measure is mightier than your treasure
When your experience is freedom
When your treasures is treasured with a Fidel Bank

Expect great things when you have a caring heart
When you have a faithful partner, a loving friend
When you have a big shoulder to learn on
Lean on fidelity

In fidelity, we lead you through the night to the light
Where the horizon is brighter
And the future is greener with pastry of prosperity

In fidelity we go the extra miles to keep a promise
We keep our words.
(March 2008)

**Written in honor of Fidelity Bank Plc for Keeping to best practice in banking and maintaining integrity in the market place.

LET'S MAKE A CHOICE

Let's make a choice
Others have gone before us
To the naughty land
Of delusion and despondency
In search of labor
In a jobless neighborhoods

Let's make a choice
Others have gone before us
After a hey in the sun
And a rain in the waters
Serving the fatherland
That has lost its fatherhood
To unconscient avarice

Let's make a choice
Before the dawn of night
Now that the morning tarries
And our strength is still great
To paddle the course of our destiny
To a glorious berth
In the virgin land of opportunities

Let's make a choice
Others have gone before us
With their wholesome hopes
Fixed on the guardian and punch
But got punctured by their
Guardian on the hard core
Of life most sublime quest

Let's make a choice
Today as we pass out
Of the rain and the sun
To pass into realms
Of higher callings
Defined by our innate
Talents, creativity and ambition

Kenn Amaechi Jnr.

To live the dreams dreamt at dawn
And walk in the beautiful visions
Of our fiery quest
To create a world, greater than the world
Of our past history and progenitors

Let's make a choice
Let's say no to vacuum vacancies
Ephemeral promises that never become
Let's make a pact with self reliance
Let's take a walk to discovery
Let's explore and explode
With the careers of our choice
For our wisdom is deep
And our knowledge light
The earth is our exploit
Our treasure is great

**Written in March, 2007, after passing out from the National Youth Service Corps (NYSC). The inspiration for this poem came after searching for a pay jobs and experiencing firsthand the futility of the search.

"The future belongs to those who see possibilities before they become obvious" – John Scully

The Quest

I AM A BANKER

I am a banker
I lay my life in servitude
To man's earnest craving
The pursuit of money.

I am a banker
I labor from sunrise to sunset
To multiply the fortune of humanity
And increase man's net worth.

I am a banker
I sleaze the poor
And swindle the laid back
And make rich the bold.

I am a banker
My bond is to take
My security is not to let
Even though my vision is to bridge
Needs and nil greed

I am a banker
I own vaults of money
But live on the wages of penny
I'm rich in sight
Because my suits, suit my lack
My neighbors, friends and family
See my affluence amidst my confluence
My confluence of wants.
(August 2012)

"In Nigeria bankers earn money but their friends and dependants and family enjoy the money. For the bankers, enjoyment is work" – Kenn Ammaechi Jnr.

Kenn Amaechi Jnr.

ME

Myself, mylife
my dreams, my future
a reflection of God's
omniscience and omnipresence
                      Me
a dedication
to the service of the Almight God
Gods creative nature
inbued in me
for the creation of a better world
through selfless service to humanity

The Quest

*to the Glory of my Creator
so help me God.*

— Kenn Amaechi Jnr.

www.ingramcontent.com/pod-product-compliance
Lightning Source LLC
Chambersburg PA
CBHW051346040426
42453CB00007B/443